Susan Wojcicki

CEO of YouTube

by Kate Moening

BLASTOFF!
2
READERS

BELLWETHER MEDIA • MINNEAPOLIS, MN

Note to Librarians, Teachers, and Parents:

Blastoff! Readers are carefully developed by literacy experts and combine standards-based content with developmentally appropriate text.

Level 1 provides the most support through repetition of high-frequency words, light text, predictable sentence patterns, and strong visual support.

Level 2 offers early readers a bit more challenge through varied simple sentences, increased text load, and less repetition of high-frequency words.

Level 3 advances early-fluent readers toward fluency through increased text and concept load, less reliance on visuals, longer sentences, and more literary language.

Level 4 builds reading stamina by providing more text per page, increased use of punctuation, greater variation in sentence patterns, and increasingly challenging vocabulary.

Level 5 encourages children to move from "learning to read" to "reading to learn" by providing even more text, varied writing styles, and less familiar topics.

Whichever book is right for your reader, Blastoff! Readers are the perfect books to build confidence and encourage a love of reading that will last a lifetime!

This edition first published in 2020 by Bellwether Media, Inc.

No part of this publication may be reproduced in whole or in part without written permission of the publisher. For information regarding permission, write to Bellwether Media, Inc., Attention: Permissions Department, 6012 Blue Circle Drive, Minnetonka, MN 55343.

Library of Congress Cataloging-in-Publication Data

Names: Moening, Kate, author.
Title: Susan Wojcicki : CEO of YouTube / by Kate Moening.
Description: Minneapolis, MN : Bellwether Media, Inc., 2020. | Series: Blastoff! Readers. Women Leading the Way | Includes bibliographical references and index. | Audience: Age 5-8. | Audience: Grades K to 3.
Identifiers: LCCN 2018053283 (print) | LCCN 2018056276 (ebook) | ISBN 9781618916754 (ebook) | ISBN 9781644871034 (hardcover : alk. paper) | ISBN 9781618917263 (pbk. : alk. paper)
Subjects: LCSH: Wojcicki, Susan–Juvenile literature. | YouTube (Electronic resource)–Biography–Juvenile literature. | Women executives–United States–Biography–Juvenile literature. | Businesspeople–United States–Biography–Juvenile literature. | Google (Firm)–Biography–Juvenile literature.
Classification: LCC TK5105.8868.Y68 (ebook) | LCC TK5105.8868.Y68 W685 2020 (print) | DDC 384.3/3 [B] –dc23
LC record available at https://lccn.loc.gov/2018053283

Editor: Al Albertson   Designer: Andrea Schneider

Printed in the United States of America, North Mankato, MN.

Table of Contents

Who Is Susan Wojcicki?

Susan Wojcicki is the **CEO** of YouTube.

It is one of the most popular web sites in the world! 1.9 billion people use YouTube every month.

YouTube headquarters

"IF YOU CAN CHANGE TECHNOLOGY, YOU CAN CHANGE THE WORLD." (2014)

Susan was born in California.
Her parents **encouraged** learning.

Susan and her sisters, Anne and Janet

California

N
W · E
S

Santa Clara
Susan's hometown

Her mom took Susan
and her sisters to the
library every week.

Getting Her Start

In college, Susan took
a **computer science** class
that changed her life.

She decided to work in **technology**.

Susan Wojcicki Profile

Birthday: July 5, 1968

Hometown: Santa Clara, California

Industry: technology

Education:
- degrees in history and literature (Harvard University)
- degree in economics (University of California, Santa Cruz)
- degree in business (University of California, Los Angeles)

Influences and Heroes:
- Esther Wojcicki (mother)
- Stanley Wojcicki (father)
- Bill Campbell (businessman)

In 1998, the owners of a new **company** called Google rented Susan's garage.

Susan realized it was a special company. She decided to join!

Google founders, Sergey Brin and Larry Page

Changing the World

Google headquarters

Susan ran **marketing** for Google. She helped the company grow quickly.

In 2014, the owners of Google put Susan in charge of YouTube!

Susan knew YouTube would succeed if **users** were happy.

People enjoyed things like music and animal videos. Susan worked to give people the videos they wanted!

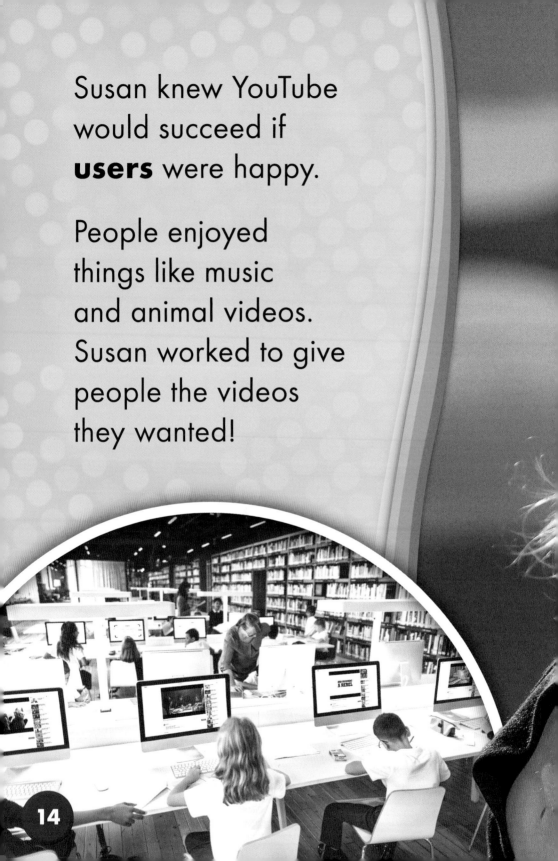

Susan with YouTube stars

People **upload** more than 400 hours of video to YouTube every minute.

Susan tries to make YouTube
safe and friendly for everyone.
It is a big **challenge**!

Susan's Future

Susan has big plans for YouTube! She wants the company to offer **virtual reality** videos.

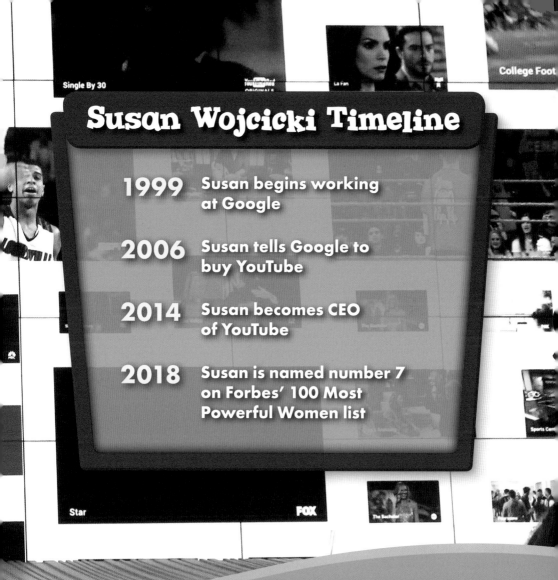

Susan Wojcicki Timeline

1999 Susan begins working at Google

2006 Susan tells Google to buy YouTube

2014 Susan becomes CEO of YouTube

2018 Susan is named number 7 on Forbes' 100 Most Powerful Women list

She also wants to open more YouTube TV stations.

Susan hopes more women will work in technology. She tries to **hire** more women to lead projects.

Susan knows that women in technology can change the world!

inside YouTube headquarters

"DREAM BIG AND TRUST THAT YOU DO HAVE THE ANSWERS." (2017)

Glossary

CEO—the highest-ranking person in a company; CEO stands for "chief executive officer."

challenge—something that is hard to do

company—a group that makes, buys, or sells goods for money

computer science—the study of computers and their uses

encouraged—gave the help needed to accomplish a goal

hire—to choose a person for a job

marketing—the activities that are involved in making people aware of a company's products

technology—the use of science to make and share useful things or to solve problems

upload—to move from a computer to a web site

users—people who use a web site

virtual reality—an environment created by a computer that people experience as real

To Learn More

AT THE LIBRARY

Lyons, Heather, and Elizabeth Tweedale. *Learn to Program*. Minneapolis, Minn.: Lerner Publications, 2017.

Owings, Lisa. *Youtube*. North Mankato, Minn.: Abdo Publishing, 2017.

Polinsky, Paige V. *Indra Nooyi: CEO of PepsiCo*. Minneapolis, Minn.: Bellwether Media, 2019.

ON THE WEB

FACTSURFER

Factsurfer.com gives you a safe, fun way to find more information.

1. Go to www.factsurfer.com.

2. Enter "Susan Wojcicki" into the search box and click 🔍.

3. Select your book cover to see a list of related web sites.

Index